Rescue the Perishing

Rescue
the
Perishing

Poems by GIBBONS RUARK

Louisiana State University Press
Baton Rouge and London
1991

Designer: Laura Roubique Gleason
Typeface: Palatino
Typesetter: Graphic Composition, Inc.
Printer and binder: Thomson-Shore, Inc.

Library of Congress Cataloging-in-Publication Data

Ruark, Gibbons.
  Rescue the perishing : poems / by Gibbons Ruark.
    p.   cm.
  ISBN 0-8071-1667-X (alk. paper). — ISBN 0-8071-1668-8 (pbk. : alk.
paper)
  I. Title.
PS3568.U17R47   1991
811'.54—dc20
                                        90-47142
                                        CIP

The author offers grateful acknowledgment to the editors of the following publications, in which poems in this book originally appeared: *Antioch Review*, "North Towards Armagh," "Transatlantic Summer Elegy"; *Coraddi*, "A Vacant Lot"; *Harvard Magazine*, "Miles from Newgrange at the Winter Solstice"; *New Criterion*, "At the Graves in Memory," "Larkin," "Wayside Flowers on the Hazel Brae"; *New Republic*, "With the Bust of Maecenas at Coole"; *New Virginia Review*, "A Change in the Weather," "Dawn Address from Kavanagh Country," "Night Flight to Dublin," "To a Countryman from Riverside"; *Pacific Review*, "Lynch"; *Ploughshares*, "Proof," "A Small Rain," "To Janey, Address Unknown," " 'What's Water but the Generated Soul?' "; *Poet and Critic*, "Wildflower Lullaby"; *Poetry*, "Postscript to an Elegy"; *Poetry Miscellany*, "To Emily, Practicing the Clarinet," "To Jennifer, Singing at the Piano"; *Poetry Northwest*, "Words to Accompany a Wildflower from Edward Thomas's Hillside"; *Raccoon*, "Glasnevin," "St. Stephen's Green"; *Salmagundi*, "Reading the Mail in Early Fall," "Words to Accompany a Small Glass Swan"; *Seattle Review*, "Last Day at Newbliss: Remembering Richard Hugo," "Leaving Hatteras," "St. Patrick's," "To an Irishman Dead Sober," "With Thanks for a Shard from Sandycove"; *Yarrow*, "Words for Unaccompanied Voice at Dunmore Head," "Words to Accompany a Photograph of Bloody Cranesbill." "Veterans" was published in a limited edition by North Carolina Wesleyan College Press. Twelve poems included here were printed as *Small Rain*, a limited-edition portfolio from the Center for Edition Works, at the State University of New York at Purchase.

Grateful thanks are owed the National Endowment for the Arts for a fellowship that generously supported work on these poems, and to Bernard and Mary Loughlin, of the Tyrone Guthrie Centre, in Ireland.

Publication of this book has been supported by a grant from the National Endowment for the Arts in Washington, D.C., a federal agency.

The paper in this book meets the guidelines for permanence and durability of the Committee on Production Guidelines for Book Longevity of the Council on Library Resources. ⊗

for my daughters

Contents

Rescue the Perishing

Postscript to an Elegy

What I forgot to mention was the desultory
Unremarkable tremor of the phone ringing
Late in the day, to say you were stopping by,
The door slung open on your breezy arrival,
Muffled car horns jamming in the neighborhood,

Our talk of nothing particular, nothing of note,
The flare of laughter in a tilted wineglass.
Or we would be watching a tavern softball game
And you would come short-cutting by, your last hard mile

Dissolving in chatter and beer on the sidelines.
How did that Yankee third baseman put it, tossing
His empty glove in the air, his old friend
Sheared off halfway home in an air crash? "I thought
I'd be talking to him for the rest of my life."

Talk as I may of quickness and charm, easy laughter,
The forms of love, the sudden glint off silverware
At midnight will get in my eyes again,
And when it goes the air will be redolent still

With garlic, a high note from Armstrong, little shards
That will not gather into anything,
Those nearly invisible flecks of marble
Stinging the bare soles of the curious
Long after the statue is polished and crated away.

Words for Unaccompanied Voice at Dunmore Head

One old friend who never writes me tells another:
The boy has need of lyrical friends around him.
Don't ask me how I ever found that out,

Given as I am to these fugitive headlands
Where not so long ago the news from Dublin
Arrived washed up with driftwood from the States,

Where the gulls rehearse the local word for weather
And then free-fall through ragged clouds to the sea wrack.
The bar at the end of the world is three miles east.

Last night the music there ascended with the smoke
From a turf fire and showered down in dying sparks
That fell on lovers and the lonely ones alike

Where they cycled the dark roads home or lingered
By a bridge till every cottage light was out—
Fell silent from the night as innocent as milkweed.

All night those soft stars burned in my watchful sleep.
At dawn I abandoned my rackety faithless car
To its own persuasions, took up a stick

And leaned uphill into the wind for the summit.
No music here but the raw alarms of seabirds
And the tireless water high against the cliff face.

No more the flute and the whiskeyed tenor rising,
The chorus of faces in the drift of smoke.
This is the rock where solitude scrapes its keel

And listens into the light for an echo.
This has to be good practice for that last
Cold wave of emptiness on whatever shore,

But why do the reckoners in my nightmares
Never ask me what I said to the speechless
Assembly of whitecaps instead of was

There anyone arm-in-arm with me as I spoke?

A Small Rain

I sit with Mick McGinn and watch the swallows
Dipping till they nearly touch the roadway.
He tells me the rain is sure to return.
A heavy sky is holding the insects down.
At evening, off the road to Annaghmakerrig,
Two horses are running, their silk flanks shining,
The pool they run by starred with water lilies.
In the hayfield beyond them the sun goes down,
And a cloud the color of pearl is building
Over the simple hills of Monaghan.
Swallows are convening in the hollows
To keep me company for the final mile.
They swoop and twitter about a small rain
Coming, or somebody sure as the rain.

St. Patrick's

Traveling light, a few scrawled notes in my pocket,
I read where floodwaters loosened Swift, great warden
Of these walls, and his rare Stella, eye sockets
Emptied of the looks of love, and tipped that burden
Up through tumbled flagstones to the instruments
Of Dr. Wilde. He calipered their topmost bones
For evidence. Heart, how the page grows dense,
Were you with me I might read without this lens.
Of tears the tiny stirrup of Swift's inner ear
That sent him raving in the Liberties,
Wilde's word that Stella's was a perfect marvel,
"Most perfect ever witnessed in a . . ."
Was it the summer lightning of your face
Made me decipher "soul" instead of "skull"?

North Towards Armagh

1

This handsome woman buying me a drink
Is a dark-haired firebrand from the Liffey's Northside.
Last night she was grilled by an Englishwoman:
"Aren't we near that 'boundary' here? Do you think
We're safe?" It's *your* fucking border, lady,
You might have the grace to know where it is.
Nearly threw the trifle in her bloodless face.
This morning, submachine guns at the ready
Covering his back, a boy from the Liverpool streets,
Burnt cork on his cheekbones, questioned my half-inch maps
Until he saw the books and souvenirs of Yeats.
Now, in all Armagh, on rainpools and barroom taps,
Windowlights, eyeglasses, slick pints of stout, the shine
Of a moment's stillness, permitting reflection.

2

The slant, rainy light through the plate-glass window
Welcomes the absence of soldiers in the street.
The publican's grim story of the car bomb
Six months back, just inches from where we sit,
Ripples through us, and we turn to our glasses.
I show her my poem for Kay and the swallows.
She mentions her recent savaging breakup,
Says nobody writes a poem without love.
"Don't you think love makes poetry possible?"
What can I say in Joe Nolan's quiet saloon,
The rain-streaked window momentarily whole,
About anything unshattered, poetry or love?
I ask her the spelling of *gelignite*.
She says it's no use in my peaceable poems.

Wayside Flowers on the Hazel Brae

Daybreak of your voice across the ocean
Swept through me like a quick wind over water
And left my longing palpable and keen.
Now I'm walking the Brae in windy weather,
Dark, then bright, then dark as the cloud shapes alter.
The vagabond wild rose blooms in the ditches,
Swaying in wind as it would float on water.
Over the next rise, a meadow of daisies
Is spotted with clover as dark as wine
Or what stipples you when you come from the shower
And lie down near me not entirely dry.
A drift of light rain falls across the air
As I walk the Brae away from you, caught
Up in flowers and the flower of my thought.

Words to Accompany a Wildflower from Edward Thomas's Hillside

Listen close and delicate:
This wildflower is the late

Wayside violet that shines
Nearly hidden in the dense

Foliage where the hills of Steep
Gave the poet pause to breathe

On his way to where the war
Changed his name into a scar,

Knocked his fine heart from his chest,
Blanked the eyes that Helen kissed.

This wild blossom still has five
Leaves of starlight, tentative,

Dried in darkness for a year
Since I found it in the far

Hillside path where Edward climbed,
Holding Helen in his mind.

Now the nameless stars are out,
Now the name of Thomas floats

Like a star among the scars.
Here's his violet for years.

Veterans

Backs to the window of the bar in Donnybrook,
Two bent but elegant soldiers remember
The Somme, living through it, how the river looked
Recalling the Liffey, the chilling number
Of wild Irish boys among the casualties.
The younger one lost an arm for his trouble;
The older, ninety-eight, first of the British
Officers to cross the Hindenburg, though able
To return intact, grows deaf to civil noise,
Yet quickens to the mention of a close
Compatriot bemedaled at the Parliament
Of London, who cheered all Dublin with his riposte:
"Insult the King and Queen? Not a bit of it boys,
Just couldn't take my eyes off the Duchess of Kent."

Dawn Address from Kavanagh Country

Black hills becoming green across the lake,
The old moon failing, I rise to first light
Troubling a mist of leaves for color, take
Thought (while it is still so early to write)
To improvise you something blue and green
And delicate enough to pay no duty,
Something contrived to fit you like the sheen
On wakening water over which three
Whoopers nudge their darlings to the rushes,
Something woven so near invisible
You might be wearing nothing as it shies
Over your shoulders, spills past credible
Lifting breasts, the riverine fall and rise
From your throat's hollow to your flaring thighs.

Words to Accompany a Small Glass Swan

1

Cold midnight, Gogarty struggling in midriver,
Having slipped the Irregulars, leaving
An aftertaste of wit and his great fur coat.
He shook himself loose from its sleeves and was off,
Promising, stroke after stroke, if he got clear
He'd give a pair of swans to the Liffey.
Today, slipping indoors out of nothing worse
Than Dublin rainfall in a minor key,
I thought of Gogarty's lost coat, the warmth
He relinquished to plunge in the freezing river,
I thought of oceanic distances,
Shelter from storm, the home fire of your face,
Then found this small clear swan along the Liffey,
And a big *duvet* as soft as Gogarty's coat.

2

Duvet, it turns out, is merely the word for down,
Not downward down but airy upward swansdown.
That last Dublin morning rose clear and cool,
Though the sky was cumulus by afternoon,
Cloud drifts more friendly than unbroken light.
Breakable swan in my pocket, I walked
Those streets where shadows came and went like water,
And then, toward evening, bent to touch a lamp's
Furled shadow, and my fingers came away wet.
The clearest glass is misted by our breathing.
Think of the way translucent loneliness
Can augur a rush of love, and you won't wonder
When this brittle, sway-necked clarity gives rise
To warmth falling on you in a cloud of down.

With the Bust of Maecenas at Coole

In this garden now without a house to care,
They quarreled or conspired beneath the hedges,
The dead whose books were all they bought of heaven.
Where the stiff-backed patroness strolled in the twenties,
A great patron's head ennobles the scene.
Once, and not from a heart too delicate
For blood's obscenities, he was so moved
Against some purge of Caesar's as to flirt
With his own beheading, flinging these words
Over the crowd still breathing in the stench
Of retribution: "Break off, butcher!"
Fast friend of poets, soldier, counselor,
West of your head a great tree stands, its coppery
Leaf cloud stirring like a thought to break off butchery.

With Thanks for a Shard from Sandycove

Late afternoon we idled on a bench
In memory of the man from Inniskeen,
The slow green water fluent beside us,

High clouds figured among leaves on the surface.
Then down along the strand to Sandycove
And the late-lit water, the sun emigrating

After a parting glance, the distant ferry
Disappearing soundlessly toward Holyhead.
We were laughing, riding the crest of company,

Your beautiful laughing wife and you and I,
When suddenly you tired of hammering
With a pebble at a stubborn boulder

And lifted it and dropped it on another
And handed me the chip that broke away.
I thought of the brute possibilities

In those farmer's hands, the place they came from,
What they might have done instead of simply
Dropping one stone on another to give

This pilgrim a shard of where he'd been.
You lifted that heaviness handily,
Keeping it briefly elevated in the air

As if more nearly the weight of a bowl
Of sacramental lather than the capstone
Of a dolmen in some field near Ballyvaughan.

Guilty as charged with a faithless penchant
For the elegiac, shy of the quick-drawn line
In the schoolyard dust, we prayed for nothing

Less than calm in the predawn hours and the laughter
Of disarming women when the hangman comes.
The sea grew dark, and then the dark was general

Over the suburbs, the window where I slept
Thrown open on the moon picking out the angle
Of a spade left leaning in a kitchen garden,

Shining like something prized from underground.

for Seamus Heaney

Leaving Hatteras

Deep summer is time forgetful of its calling,
The place a screened porch hugging the home Atlantic,
My brother's voice beside me: All you do is close
Your eyes. The surf's invisible below the dunes,
But its sound is the fallback and lift of memory.

After the days of heat and stillness, heat piling
Over our heads in columns ranked immovable,
The storm-cooled breezes riffle every window shade,
Freshness billows and flaps the air like a sail.
All I do is close my eyes. A screen door shudders
And bangs and a boy lights out for the water

And it is south of here by thirty years and more
Where the shore curls inward and the dunes are lower
And a boy can see his father from the water
Cleaning and oiling his tackle in a porch chair.
By the time he gets it right the fish will vanish.

One afternoon he walks as far as the shell line
Marking the tide's reach, remembers his scaling knife,
And goes back in and puts his feet up for a minute
And wakes to a plate of oysters on the table.
Now on a sleeping-porch just wavering toward its name
My brother and I are pulling on our road clothes

Halfheartedly, a sleeve or a sock at a time,
As if we were young and moving house all over
And not just going home at the end of summer.
There is a snapshot of a kindred moment somewhere,
More formal, though we stand there in our undershorts,

August in Carolina laving our faces,
The sun through stained glass dim but unrelenting.
It is the choir room before my sister's wedding,
My father reaching to help us with our cuff links,
His brow lit with sweat or the new forgetfulness.
Here what looks like water shivers over the screens

And we breathe deep, two of us only, buttoning
Our sleeves and zipping up the nylon duffel bags,
Unless you count the lazybones in the doorway,
Stretching himself and rubbing his eyes with his knuckles,
Blinking like a child as the room turns familiar.

At the Graves in Memory

The land there rolls no more than the quiet river
Curves. Drifts of pine straw resin the ground.
Summer is remembered like a wild fever

That left the forehead when the sun went down.
That February day was mild as Easter.
There to the west of my abandoned town,

Shirt-sleeved gravediggers smoked at a corner
Of lawn unbroken by an upright stone.
Soft wind in the pines, the sound of water

Stilled in memory, the merciful brief drone
Of the old liturgy, and it was over.
My mother's body by my father's bones.

Winter. Easter weather. Long gone life-givers.
The land there rolls no more than the quiet river.

Transatlantic Summer Elegy

Dusk in Kinvara. An old man quietly sings
To the air. In a distant time zone, late summer
Is leaving town. From houses with small children,
The yellow porch lights flick on after supper,
Hazy constellations of dim low stars.
High stars are still, the air so still the odor
Of honeysuckle sleeps in the hedges.
This is a night to keep still in the branches
Till someone on a porch starts calling you home.
Each house circled by light is holding its breath
When suddenly out of nowhere a breeze rises
And the whole of the great night tree starts swaying
As if it were not all the leaves but one.
The wrong old man keeps singing in Kinvara.

To Emily, Practicing the Clarinet

Early this morning, acres of birdsong
In the rising light. Now, as if still not
Dried out after dewfall, a quavering
Throaty note, and then another, from out
Beyond the hedgerow, or even across
The water, the cool reed-and-water strains
Of a young girl dreaming into the mouthpiece
Of a clarinet. Sometimes, my quick flame
Of a daughter, you lay down your instrument,
Are sassy, knowing, and brimful of banter,
But when those throaty notes rise from the earth
I hear you practicing as if your breath
Floating over that reed were innocent
Of the great empty air it has to enter.

To Jennifer, Singing at the Piano

Here the silence, though peacefully broken
By birds or a fresh wind over the lake,
Can feel like a skein of loneliness shaken
Out over me musing into the late
Glow of a long evening, waiting for dark
To sleep. There the music, where you sit playing
And singing, thousands of miles south and westward,
Where the dark comes on in earlier evening,
There the music chastens the dark. You were
Always the quiet one, your hand at the nape
Of your neck for meaning, or your eyes that flare,
But now I hear you lightly singing, daughter,
As I slip gratefully off to sleep,
That tremulous "Bridge over Troubled Water."

"What's Water but the Generated Soul?"

You have lost weight from the days of walking
And are up before others in the house
To step through mist and rhododendron bulking
The path that winds down to the lake. Curlews
Flash and cry and skim the rippled surface.
The leaves, the scattered movement of the leaves,
And then, again, a stillness resembling peace.
What's loneliness but movement in the leaves?
From the house uphill the smell of turf smoke
Follows the mist into the upper air.
Hidden in a stand of reeds, the small boat
Tilts in its sleep and ships a little water.
Rowed slowly and quietly, it will still float
What rises in you to the other shore.

Larkin

This first-name-only business beggars history,
As if the young mistook Ben Jonson's need
To keep a certain name immaculate
Till darkness tugged his wrist in the graveyard road.

Nearsighted and too far-off to wax familiar,
I would indulge the old formality
Of last names, since the man sank to his last hour
An ocean from my windows, low or high.

Larkin it is, then, with an added Philip
For those who would distinguish "English poet"
From, say, "hero of the Dublin shipyards."
His road was a hero's byway, but he knew it.

Larkin I have been reading now since sunrise,
Or rather, with the day thus clouded over,
Morning. His trains on sidings, his racehorses
Nuzzling the dusk, his taking the measure

Of rainfall while we still look for a cloud,
His chosen solitude, a singular light
Dispensed by water in a lifted tumbler,
A real day's shouldered and delivered freight.

"This is not the full portion of whiskey,"
I muttered, young and tanked on Dylan Thomas,
But now his angle's undeniable.
Somebody, somewhere, is breaking a promise.

Surefooting through the rain of rice and horn blare
Flattering some lovely daughter's wedding ride,
His tune is brassy, muted, grave, and just—
Jelly Roll's "Dead Man Blues" as the slow hearse glides.

Or think of it this way, as *L* for Larkin
Enters its cold-water flat in England's
Alphabet: Just now I was leaning forward,
His closed *High Windows* thin between my hands,

Palm to bare palm were it not for the poetry.
Knock in a nail and hang that image somewhere
Out of the way. Call it, should you think of it,
A man contemplating applause or prayer.

Night Flight to Dublin

Through the night, beyond the glazed monocle
Dulling the infinite, the wings' freight shudders
And turns the air to jetstream. I'm muttering
With a penlight over some chronicle
Of Ulster, a small hovering circle
Of false dawn panning the names of slaughtered
Chieftains, of treacherous wives who uttered
The knife words piously as oracles . . .
Set down at last, my nerve ends are a shaky
Foreigner's, I'm traveling unarmed.
Fear smokes the walls of these shadowy quarters.
May she I lately slept with rise unharmed.
The pub's cracked mirror says the clouds are breaking,
The faces friendly, not one of them hers.

St. Stephen's Green

"There in the gardens you will find the Yeats
Memorial by Henry Moore," a blade
Of greening bronze so rooted by its weight
In stone the worst wind ever to invade
This island could not tear it into flight
Or set it whirling like a weather vane.
Across the plaque some punk has sloshed in white
The tribute of the moment: PUNKS. The rains
Have left it legible. Beyond the swans,
The young, their bodies groaning with their lips,
Are deaf to birdsong in their tiny earphones.
As an old pal put it shrewdly in his cups:
He strove to love them in the old high mode;
Urgent, they want to do it in the road.

To an Irishman Dead Sober

Dear ghost, I don't blame you for casting the fisheye
On this fantastic island, precipitous
With drink and kinsmen conspiring to pry
Your company away from those few spacious
Wintry hours you thanked for returning your soul
To you. Still, the sorriest wandering hours
Are history, and we might note the toll
They take, however grim. Forgive me, years
Ago, though it is painful now to say it,
We laughed ourselves lost in a ground fog of booze
And came to singing badly, two-man riot
In the night-dark Ladies' Room. What made you choose
To rally us, though your throat was whiskey raw,
From Synge's to Adam's curse without a flaw?

To a Countryman from Riverside

One night we roared off-key through half of Galway.
The night before, late twilight in the lees
Of our Jamesons, we played the gulls to every
Toothless raconteur the boys would send our way.
Tonight this quayside pub consoles me lonely
Where we clanked our glasses to the last words
Of our fathers, neither man of them loony
Enough to hear us out, deaf graves absurd
As our infernal nightlong argument
Over the mileage from London to Oxford,
Or was it the other direction we went?
Our forefathers' pikes clashed at some bloody ford.
Had we not wrangled and come out of it brothers,
No doubt by now we would have killed each other.

Lynch

What's left of the day is dark and wayward
As the barman's story, raw weather rolling
From the islands, oracular, secretive
Voice idling back and forth along the bar.
"Strange as it sounds, it was the lad's own father
Hanged him, never set foot in the streets again.
Mayor of Galway he was, Fitzstephen
Lynch, the very year your man Columbus
Prayed for safe passage there in St. Nicholas.
The lad young Walter killed was Juan Gomez,
Guest of the house, trusted to the mayor's hands,
Who could force no Galway man to knot the rope."
Out in the streets the dark grows medieval,
Rain blurs the faces of the city's clocks,

And out beyond the breakers by the Spanish wall,
Travel-sore, weary, young Juan is writing home.
"It was a harsh crossing, Father, scarcely
An hour's abatement in the storm, and hard
Hunger in the end, racking wind could snap
A timber driving us for days from harbor
Till we fell back hugging the northerly
Coastline nearly as we could, the sea calming
Once just long enough to sluice overboard,
Tatters for a flag, scant ceremony
Croaked at the railing, a young seaman's body
Got caught in the rigging and drowned on board,
Before tonight the only man of us
Not cold to the bone and white with hunger,

Your friend my benefactor Mister Lynch
Insisting, evenhanded as the storm,
On doling out the last hard scraps of tack
To merchant's son and cabin boy alike.
Last night we tossed to sleep in a hailstorm,
Slung against the bulkheads in our hammocks
Till not one of us but cried for landfall
And was washed up by a daybreak brilliant
On so calm a sea we thought to have died
Until a bird cawed and we saw the smoke
Erect as a mainmast in the stillness
Rise up heavenward from a cottage thatch.
The captain and the night had found us shelter.
Daylight glazed the water like a slow cow

Ruminant and stone-still in the distance.
Inishbofin. Island of the White Cow.
We had come to in her protected harbor.
The islanders here have little to spare,
A few small oatcakes and some bitter ale,
But they are kind and what they have is ours.
The smoke of turf is pungent in the room.
A child of the place is drowsing at my knee.
An older boy, perhaps of an age with me,
Is warbling away on some kind of flute.
It has the sweetest sound, and now the sound
Of wind has almost died out in my ears.
Drink and the fire are pulling me to sleep.
I will write you the end of this in Galway."

Reading the Mail in Early Fall

A small leafstorm of correspondences:

This gift book from a musical Welsh girl
Whose dark head launched a dozen seminars.
Somebody *else's* poems! and not the inward furl
Of lines by one more gloomy narcissistic sister,
But a woman's whole words for her dead and living men.
She writes her friend Tu Fu beyond the mountain
That she relishes the low-salt meat of monogamy,
Mild afternoons of wine in her own back yard,
Yet still she crosses herself and a continent
To come bedecked in clouds of scent and jewelry
To an old friend dying in a cancer ward,
Loved at long last by beautiful women.
He looks up lightheaded from his heaviest body,
Then shoves off eastward in the untied boat of Po Chu-i.

And this, what's this? A two-inch-tall giraffe,
All thanks to the slender elegant neck
And tilted head, the savvy contagious laugh
And the soft quick look away from heartbreak.
Little wooden long-neck nosing the leafless air,
Your frail crosshatch of stripes is scarcely visible
In the emptiness that shoulders your pure
Upward longing there on the polished table.
Brief shadowing shape of the coming loneliness,
Young woman who could wake up Robert Herrick,
What gives? I'll never know but luck would be my guess.
This creature's intricate as the strayed fawn at the salt lick
Or an Oriental silence, and nearly
Small enough to carry with me when I die.

I light the fire for tea, but it's not over.
Here's the mailman back with a packet he missed:
Leaf after glossy leaf, the face and figure
Of my daughter under the strange light of the East.
Here she is at her desk in the schoolhouse
Amid the upturned interrogative looks.
And here the question in her own lit face
Is not to be plumbed in the deepest of books.
In this one she and Kikko in Shizuoka
Are being Chubby Checker, hip to hip,
And here her gaze is blue and brimmed as the ocean.
I lift this smoky early-morning tea
To the brightness that falls from flowering young women,
For once spilling nothing between the cup and the lip.

To Janey, Address Unknown

Wherever you are, the coast is tumbled stone,
And there in the clearing is a white-tailed deer.
Listening a moment to these words alone,
Perhaps you will believe the silence here.
This morning as I stand still on the lawn
An owl halloos somewhere beyond the meadow,
Beyond the boundary, and then is gone.
The swan unfurls above his brilliant shadow.
Here where he wavers in the sun's return
To inland water, we might just gather
Our thoughts toward a word or two, or take turns
Saying simply nothing of the weather.
Meanwhile, if you listen from your far wherever,
Silence where I am will include a deer.

Last Day At Newbliss: Remembering Richard Hugo

In the early afternoon, a fine rain falls
To three clocks ticking, not one of them on time.
Outside, the wet road goes nowhere but Cootehill.
One local pilgrim, after years of longing,
Finally made it to Lourdes. Asked how he found
It, he said he took the Castleblayney road.
Towns and the names of towns, wet roads going nowhere
But Cootehill, the way to Lourdes through Castleblayney,
If a friend coughs up the money for the fare.
Otherwise we are left with rainy weather,
More salutary, sure, than no weather at all.
To give me leave to remember you clearly,
Miss Annie McGinn of Newbliss delivers
A dark pint slow and silent as the island rain.

Glasnevin

A chance of summer in the Liffey air,
We drove through Northside at the holy hour
To walk among gravestones at Glasnevin,
Parnell, Maud Gonne MacBride, *diversi santi* . . .
In Ulster, just as the year was flowering,
The Sten guns roared and adamant hymn singers
Slumped in their bloody pews, and now, rung off
This granite, the old staunch hymns are streaming
From the country churches of my boyhood.
With all the Republican dead so near,
Our guide the begrudger, calling Hopkins
"The convert," leads us first to the inventor
Of plastic surgery, as well he might,
These days of the gelignite ascendancy.

The Enniskillen Bombing

Remembrance Day, 1987

"Showery with bright periods," said the forecast,
The way it does so many days in Ireland,
And indeed the arrowy soft rain fell

And the clouds parted more often than not
Above that watery parish, and the farmer
Walked in collarless from Derrygore,

The butcher left his awning snug against the lintel,
Two boys forgot their caps on the orchard wall.
Nobody looking at the sky or listening

To the weather would ever have predicted
That thunder would erupt before the lightning,
Blow the whole end gable of St. Michael's out

And bring the roof spars raining piecemeal down—
Not the slow-tempered grocer gone open-mouthed
With or without a cry as the windows roared,

Not the stooped pharmacist red-faced with grief,
Not the veteran of two World Wars in all
His ribbons, scrabbling with his raw bare hands

Through the choking dust for anybody's heartbeat,
Not the father wandering almost blindly,
Eyebrows seared from his face, who found his son

Still breathing only to knock the tip of his stick
Against his daughter's wedding ring, her splintered
Hand upturned in the rubble incarnadine

As the fuchsia banking a rain-swept roadside.

Before It Happened

One afternoon a friend from the Falls and I
Drove out from Sligo into Enniskillen
For a quiet drink among old lamps and mirrors,

The glancing talk conspiratorial
As wives at the half-doors, silences freighted,
Lamplight pooled with sunlight on the polished bar,

The street outside a cleared-out Control Zone.
Across the street and up the narrow stair,
In a room with spring light swimming in the windows,

Fine as lace and firm as Blake's engravings,
The paintings of a dozen Irish wildflowers,
One after one, hung cleanly on the wall.

My friend the country walker, botanizer
Reared in the gutted streets of West Belfast,
Called every one by name from memory.

Bogbean, pipewort, grass of Parnassus,
Harebell looking so fragile it might tatter
In a breeze, yet stubborn as the stone ones

High on the capitals at Corcomroe.
We came downstairs into the slant of evening
And drove away in the unmolesting dark.

As we left behind the small lights of the town,
The voice at the wheel was naming constellations,
Orion, Cassiopeia, where they wavered

At first, then spread their nets of stars in the night wind.

A Change in the Weather

Last midnight I walked in the hawthorn lane,
Hearing no sound, the scrap of moon so vivid
The night sky shone transparent as the day.
Suddenly I trembled at the slow lucid
Unfolding days I had such longing for.
What if the sky forgets to change, dawns clear
And clear till there is neither time nor weather?
How could you fly to me through changeless air?
Toward morning, the moon burned orange, then cloud
On cloud passed over till it was darkened,
And now this morning rain. Surely if so soft
A rain can out of nowhere cloud the broken
Moon while I am sleeping, so you can softly
Come and brush my waking eyelids with your mouth.

One for the Birds

On a May morning before I left you
I lay awake this early and listened
To dim birds questioning the dark for music.
Here and there a single sparrow wakened.
You breathed beside me, the air as moist
With promise as the glimmering dawn of rain
On this island, names of these trees still lost
In the lake fog, names of these birds unknown.
Under what stars did I dream you scattering
Bread crumbs to the dove's low-throated lonesome flute?
Bright bird of my lifetime, fresh May morning,
Carolina chickadee, for you I wrestle
My heaviness till it flies off like dew
At daybreak or lights where the redbreast whistles.

Proof

You helped me stow these pages in a knapsack,
Tossed me a blessing, "Do sit near the wings,"
And I was airborne. Small hours of panic
Now dissolved in birdsong, your look at parting
Lights my work desk under an Ulster roof.
The book I gave you is dead manuscript,
Say the grim instructions for reading proof.
To touch it is to desecrate a crypt.
Today's slight changes rung, I am lifting
A glass to your green eyes beyond the waters,
Hearing in a country house well inland
The pitch and rub of ancient voices, sifting
That strange surf for whether or how it matters
To write down green eyes with a dying hand.

Wildflower Lullaby

All day out wandering the high limestone
For brief scarves of radiance in the crevices
Has deepened into sundown that will ease
Toward darkness and a sleep I'll call my own.
All day the dull gray bluffs so seemingly bare
Have yielded the gentians' small cerulean
Stars, bright trefoil, and the fair mountain avens.
Light was in their petals and I left it there.
Now the sun flames out in the blue half-moon
Of Galway Bay just visible, the night
Leans toward me humming its old tune, "Sleep Forever,"
And some perennial, say the earth's own thought
Of you, assumes its common name and starts to flower
Like sea thrift springing upward from a cleft in stone.

Words to Accompany A Photograph
of Bloody Cranesbill

Long as morning lived in the windy meadow
We looked for nothing but the feathery solo

Flares of May wildflowers blowing among the stones.
Cloud shadows came and mottled the hillside, and once

We looked up to a sail blue and particular
As gentian tilting toward Aran in the harbor,

But just as quickly bent back to the tufted grass
And were lost again to the depths and distances.

Flower after isolate flower sprang from that ground,
And then a pair that leaned and riffled in the wind,

One shying closed as the fingers are seen to close
When gathered at the lips for a breath-blown kiss,

The other soaked through with light and wholly open
As your eyes when something is about to happen.

Here they are, the nicked petals and faintly furred stems
Of bloody cranesbill, crimson-veined geraniums

We found collecting only the daylight's shimmer
On the wildflower bank of a clear conversant river

While the high sea scattered the cliffs with a bloom of foam.

Miles from Newgrange at the Winter Solstice

The long-lit landscape of the summer solstice
Just over our heads, we stood in a seamless
Darkness. I touched your hand to the carved stone
Like some deep negative of Braille, each crevice

The whorl of a mind now wordless and flown.
Outside, the long shine on the river ran,
Shadows mingled, and a sudden fish leapt
And fell back scattering its reflection.

I heard the tenderness of your taken breath,
Felt for your hand again, and out we crept
Into the smell of mown hay and daylight,
Those stones left weighing the silence they kept.

Summer ended. Leaves fell. Now the window's white
With flurries or the full moonlight of late
December, we're too fleshed with desire to tell.
Beyond the waters, beyond the dark, light

Makes its once-a-year move down a channel
Intelligence left in the tumulus wall,
And while we lie together close as a fever
On childish limbs, it glosses for a still

Second a text as fine as a feather.
After long love, we should let dawn discover
The crevices between us, so we might not lie
Underground unread and dark forever.

A Vacant Lot

One night where there is nothing now but air
I paused with one hand on the banister
And listened to a film aficionado's
Careless laughter sentence poetry to death.

It's twenty gone years and a few poems later,
The house demolished, the film man vanished,
The friend who introduced us to him dead.

I side with one old master who loves to tell
His film-buff friends that film is *like* an art form,
And yet my eyes keep panning the empty air
Above the rubble, as if, if I could run

The film back far enough, I might still start
For home down the darkened street from the newsstand
And turn a corner to the house still standing,

A faint light showing in an upstairs window.
Is someone reading late? Or is it the night
Our newborn lies burning up with fever,
And all the doctor can say is plunge her

In cold water, wrap her up and hold her,
Hold her, strip her down and plunge her in again
Until it breaks and she is weak but cooling?

Is it the night they call about my father
And I lay the mismatched funeral suit
In the back seat with the cigarettes and whiskey
And drive off knowing nothing but Death and South?

Somewhere a tree limb scrapes at a gutter.
The wind blows. Late trucks rattle the windows.
Never you mind, I say out loud to the girls

Away at school, There's nothing there to hurt you.
The sky is thickening over a vacant lot,
And when I leave there is a hard rain drumming
With the sound of someone up in the small hours,

Thirsty, his palm still warm from a sick child's
Forehead, running the spigot in the kitchen
Full force till the water's cold enough to drink.